A·HUNDRED·FABLES·OF ÆSOP

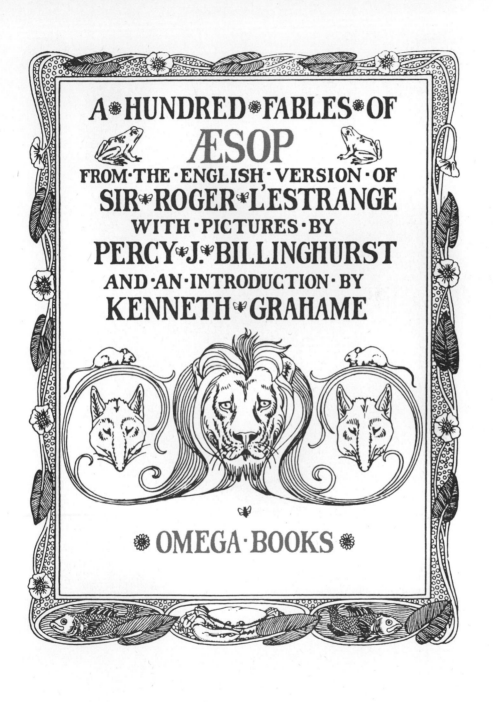

A · HUNDRED · FABLES · OF
ÆSOP
FROM · THE · ENGLISH · VERSION · OF
SIR · ROGER · L'ESTRANGE
WITH · PICTURES · BY
PERCY · J · BILLINGHURST
AND · AN · INTRODUCTION · BY
KENNETH · GRAHAME

OMEGA · BOOKS

This edition published 1984 by Omega Books Ltd,
1 West Street, Ware, Hertfordshire,
and copyright © Omega Books Ltd 1984

ISBN 1 85007 045 8

Printed and bound in Finland by K.J. Gummerus Osakeyhtiö.

INTRODUCTION.

The fable had its origin, we are given to understand, in a germ of politeness still lingering in the breasts of the superior, or preaching, portion of humanity, who wished to avoid giving more pain than necessary when pursuing the inevitable task laid upon them by their virtues, of instructing the inferior and silent portion how to be—well, just a little less inferior, if they would only listen patiently to what they were told. It was also frankly admitted by many, that there were difficulties in getting a frivolous humanity to listen at all, unless one took a leaf from the book of that unprofitable rascal the story-teller, a spinner of webs for the sheer irridescence and gossamer-film and sparkle of the dainty thing itself; with no designs whatever upon fat, black flies to be caught and held in its meshes. And so, with half a sigh, the preacher fell upon the element of fiction, and the fable was born.   It would have been pleasanter, of course, to have told Smith to his face what a rogue he was, and Jones, what an idiot everybody thought him ; but unfortunately there was no means of putting compulsion on Smith and Jones to attend. Again, it would have been quite easy to have got the Smiths and Joneses to sit round in a circle, while the theme was the folly of Robinson and the roguery of Jenkins ; but Jenkins and Robinson might stroll in, arm-in-arm, in the middle, and the preacher who aimed at being a popular success knew that he must not only avoid all little unpleasant-nesses, but also spin a web whose meshes were fine enough to catch and to hold, without undue obvious-ness, flies of every bulk, from Smith down to the recalcitrant Jenkins.

It is more probable that the thing had its roots in the fixed and firm refusal of the community from its very beginning, to allow any one of its members to go about calling any other one a fool or a rogue, "of his own mere notion." If anybody has got to be put away for folly, or trounced for roguery, society has always told off some one to do it, and paid him a more or less adequate salary. The amateur has never been recognised nor countenanced, and though occasionally he may score a success for the moment, and set a convicted people beating their breasts in the streets, confessing their sins to each other at the street-corners, and making piles of their costly books and curios and precious ornaments in the market-place, sooner or later the old rule asserts itself, the paid policeman moves you on as before, and the forsaken and discredited amateur comes to hopeless grief.

What then was to be done? The inadequate policeman had to be supplemented, the amateur must somehow say his say. There was a certain moral cowardice in the means he hit upon. The friendly, tactful, unobstrusive beasts around him— could they not be seized upon and utilised to point the requisite moral? True, it would be no good to hold up their real characteristics for the public admonishment. The moment they were really studied they were seen to be so modest, so mutually helpful, so entirely free from vanity, affectation, and fads; so tolerant, uncomplaining, and determined to make the best of everything ; and, finally, such adepts in the art of minding their own business, that it was evident a self-respecting humanity would not stand the real truth for a moment.   But one could deal out the more prominent of human failings among them ; one could agree, for argument's sake, that the peacock was to be vain, the wolf unregardful of his plighted word, the jackdaw a snob with a weakness for upper circles ; and the thing was done.   The Smiths and Joneses, instead of disputing the premisses, fell into the trap ; while the honest beasts, whose characters were thus meanly filched from them, instead of holding indignation-meetings, and passing resolutions of protest, as they might have done had they been merely human, took the nobler course of quietly continuing to mind their own business.

But though they acquiesced and submitted, it must not be thought that they did not feel and resent, very keenly indeed, the ungentlemanly manner in which they had been exploited, for moral purposes, by people with whom they only wished to live in mutual esteem and respect in a world in which *there was plenty of room for both.   When you meet a bird or a beast, and it promptly proceeds to move off, in an obviously different direction, without abuse indeed, or scurrility, or even reproach, but with a distinct intention of seeing as little of you as possible during the rest of the afternoon, you may be pretty sure it is thinking of Æsop's Fables.   If only somebody would withdraw and apologise, and arrange that things should be on the same footing as before!*

Some beasts have gone so far as to take a leaf out of the book of the fabulist, and compile a volume of their own.   Though humanity had behaved in a way to which they themselves would have scorned to stoop, that was no reason (they argued) why they should shun any moral lesson that was to be picked up, even from Man.   A beast's life is so short, so eventful and precarious, that he is never above learning, never too proud to take a hint; more than all, he never thinks that what he dosn't know isn't worth knowing.   I was allowed a glimpse at the book one afternoon, in a pine wood, when the world was hot and sleepy, and the beasts had dined well.   But I could not get permission to take it away, and, as I was sleepy too, I can only half recollect a scant fable or two out of that rich treasure-house ; and somehow I have never been able to happen upon that pine wood again.

Naturally enough with creatures who live by rule and order and inherited precept, the inconsequential and irregular habits of man afford much food for beast-reflection. Here is a fable (by a monkey apparently) which touches on this puzzling aspect of humanity.

THE APE AND THE CHILD IN THE LEGHORN HAT.

A frolicsome ape, who in much careless ease inhabited a lordly mansion in Regent's Park, lounged up one afternoon to certain bars, on the other side of which selected specimens of humanity were compelled to promenade each day for the instruction and diversion of philosophic apes. A little maid in a Leghorn hat having timidly approached the bars, her large fat mother, shaking her imperiously by the shoulder, ordered her to observe the pitty ickle monkey, so mild and so gentle, and give it a piece of her bun at once, like a good, kind, charitable ickle girl. The small maiden, though herself extremely loth, proffered her bun to the ape, who possessed himself of it with a squeal of delight, and bit her finger to the bone as well : for he had bitten nothing more juicy and succulent than a neighbour's tail for a whole week past; and tails are but gristly things at the best. But the large, fat mother, falling upon the already shrieking little girl, shook and cuffed her unmercifully, protesting that of all the naughty, tiresome, self-willed little trollops, and that never, never, never would she take her a-pleasuring again.

MORAL.

Parents of the human species have an altogether singular and unaccountable method of rearing their young. Yet they grow up somehow, nevertheless, and often become quite good and useful citizens : so there may be something in it, and it's a lesson to us not to be proud and think we know everything.

Here is another (by a dog this time) based on the same characteristic, but written from a slightly different and more doggy point of view.

THE DOG, THE CHILD, AND THE MOON.

A child sat on the nursery floor and cried for the moon, which was shining so temptingly through the window. A conscientious dog who was strolling by, and had been wanting sorely to bay the moon all the evening, because he had a bad pain in his inside that kept telling him to do it, only he was mighty afeared of being kicked, sat down beside the infant, and, with the sole remark that circumstances were too strong for him, lifted his snout. Then the night was filled with music, till even the face of the moon wore a pained expression; and the dog felt the pain in his inside trickling away through his ribs. Attracted by the outcry, the mother hastened to the room, and smacked the child soundly for its folly and unreasonableness. But she patted and praised the dog, who was sitting severely on his tail, and called him a noble, sympathetic fellow, who could not see others in trouble without being moved to share their distress. Then the dog swaggered out of the room feeling good all over, and resolving that next morning he would dig a hole in the geranium-bed large enough to bury the moon itself.

MORAL.

You never can tell with exactness how human beings will act, under any conditions. Therefore when you want to howl at the moon, or do anything contraband, badly enough, better go and do it and get it over. You can but be kicked, and you probably won't be, and you will get rid of the bad pain in your inside.

Then there was that fable—and the one about—and the other one where—and then that very naughty one which—but it is time to pull up, as I promised faithfully not to. How it all comes back to me as I write! The cushion of moss and pine-needles, the song of the streamlet hard by, the squirrel perched half-way up a tree-trunk and chattering, "Do read him that one about—" and the jay, who *was turning over the leaves, looking round and saying, "O you shut up! This is my copy he's looking at, and it opens at all the right places!" The rabbits sat round in a ring, silent and large-eyed, with just a flicker passing over their ever-unrestful noses. They will always come to listen to a story, however old and hackneyed, and never open their mouths except to say, " Now another, please!" The badger, who, as the biggest member present, ought to have been doing the honours, and knew it, sat and scratched himself, and looked crossly at the jay. He wanted to say something cutting, but knew the jay was his master at repartee. Then the woodland muttered its spell, and a drowsiness crept over us. When I awoke the badger's chair was vacant, the rabbits were but a rustle in the bracken, the squirrel and the jay but a quiver in a tree-top and a glint of blue against a distant copse.*

Well! The story-teller, the gossamer-web-spinner, has come to his own by this time, and the fabulist, who started with such a flourish, has long ceased to mount his tub. Even while these very fables were in course of writing, the axe was being laid to the root of the tree, and a whimsical fellow, with his tongue in his cheek, was compiling the " Arabian Nights" In this matter humanity, though just as liable as the individual to its temporary fits of affectation, knows what it wants and sees that it gets it, and never troubles to justify its selection by argument. Did it care to do so, it might contend that people, by diligent attention to morals and rubbing in of applications, had become quite too good for anything, and the fables had done their work so thoroughly that now the time had arrived for a little relaxation, honestly earned. Or it might argue, on the other hand, that the job had proved too tough a one, that the story which posed as an obvious index to personal conduct had got to be a bore and a nuisance, and that it was much nicer to be frankly bad and shameless and abandoned, and read fiction. But humanity, in the mass, never argues—and rightly ; and the reader can please himself with whichever theory he likes, sure of this at least, that the story henceforth will be tolerated only for itself, that the fable has had its day and ceased to be.

But a method may expire, and its output yet remain that undefined thing, attained by neither prayer nor fasting—a classic. (Indeed, so long as you are a part of this earth's old crust, you must generally wait till you are a stratum before people will begin paying attention to you and calling you nice names.) There are in literature men, women, and beasts, who survive owing to fidelity in portraiture to the natural type. There are equally men, women, and beasts, who live from their very deviation from the real thing—fresh and captivating creations with rules of their own. These are the folk who people the world of fairy-tale, heraldry, and fable; and many such village communities flourish in classic-land. Vitality—that is the test; and, whatever its components, mere truth is not necessarily one of them. A dragon, for instance, is a more enduring animal than a pterodactyl. I have never yet met any one who really believed in a pterodactyl; but every honest person believes in dragons—down in the back-kitchen of his consciousness. And every honest person believes that the fable-people exist, or existed, somewhere—not on this planet, perhaps, since personal experience must be allowed its place when evidence has to be weighed, but—well, the Census Department has never yet overhauled the Dog-Star.

And this classic is here given forth in the brave old seventeenth-century version of Sir Roger L'Estrange, who wrote, by a happy gift, in the very language (we feel sure) that the Fable-beasts now talk among themselves in Fable-land. Modern renderings, with one eye on the anxious parent and the other on the German governess, have often achieved an impotence of English that increases our admiration of a tongue that can survive such mis-handling, and still remain the language of men. "Insipid Twittle-Twattles," to use L'Estrange's own phrase. A Royalist politician and a fluent and copious pamphleteer, he had graduated in the right school for work wherein one hard-hitting word must needs supply the place of whole page or long-drawn paragraph in the less restricted methods by which the human conscience now insists on being approached. In the sad case of the Lion, the Bear, and the Fox, a modern version draws the moral in these satisfactory if hardly stimulating terms:

"*Those who fight with each other lose all, and give others the chance of enriching themselves.*"

Dear me, do they really? Lay this alongside of our politician's, and with a snap and a bite he has you by the leg.

"*'Tis the fate of all* Gotham Quarrels, *when fools go together by the ears, to have knaves run away with the stakes.*"

Again,—" *A certain Jackdaw was so proud and ambitious that, &c.,*" bleats and trickles our modern version. "*A Daw that had a mind to be sparkish,*" says L'Estrange, saving his breath for his story. Yet he is not merely forcible, terse, and arresting. With what a prettiness of phrase he puts (in his preface) the case for the Fable! "*What cannot be done by the dint of Authority, or Persuasion, in the Chappel, or in the Closet, must be brought about by the Side-Wind of a Lecture from the Fields and the Forrests.*" And there is a touch both quiet and appealing in his account of the Tailless Fox, and his efforts to get level again with

Society : " . . . But however, for the better countenance of the scandal, he got the Master and
Wardens of the Foxes Company to call a Court
of Assistants, where he himself appeared, and
made a Learned Discourse upon the Trouble,
the Uselessness, and the Indecency, of Foxes wearing
Tails."

But, as I have said, it is in his Beast-talk that
our politician (naturally enough) excels :

" But as they were entering upon the Dividend,
' Hands off,' says the Lion. ' This part is mine by
the Privilege of my Quality ; this, because I'll
have it in spite of your Teeth ; this, again, because
I took most pains for't ; and if you dispute the
Fourth, we must e'en Pluck a Crow about it.'" In
the " Wolf and the Lamb," " ' Nay,' says t'other,
' you'll never leave your chopping of Logick, till
your Skin's turned over you Ears, as your Father's
was, a matter of Six Months ago, for prating at
this sawcy rate.'"

L'Estrange may have had his faults of diction :
faults of excess, of violence, of recurrent effort for
the explosive phrase, wherein we get, indeed, the

telling snapshot effect, but somehow hear the click of the Kodak as well. Yet his version remains the one version, and these are not the times in which we may expect to get another. It is more than doubtful whether Æsop would have approved of it ; and yet, for good or for evil, it is the ultimate version !

Those green back-garden doors that lead to the trim classic plots—they are opened but rarely now-a-days ! For they are a trifle warped, and their paint swollen, and they stick and jam, and one can find neither time nor effort for the necessary tug. But once inside this particular door—if one takes the pains—how one is possessed by the inhabitants, their surroundings, their ways, and their points of view ! Emerging, one really expects to meet them at every corner, to be hailed by them, to put the natural question and get the appropriate answer. One forgets, for the moment, that the real four-legged or feathered fellows one encounters are sullen, rancorous, and aggrieved—have a book of their own, in fine, a version in which it is we who point the moral and adorn the tale !

KENNETH GRAHAME.

CONTENTS

CONTENTS.

A HUNDRED FABLES OF

ÆSOP

FABLE I.

The Cock and the Jewel.

AS a *Cock* was turning up a Dunghill, he spy'd a *Jewel*. Well (says he to himself) this sparkling Foolery now to a Lapidary in my place, would have been the Making of him; but as to any Use or Purpose of mine, a *Barley-Corn* had been worth Forty on't.

The Moral.

He that's Industrious in an Honest Calling, shall never fail of a Blessing. 'Tis the part of a Wise Man to Prefer Things Necessary before Matters of Curiosity, Ornament, or Pleasure.

THE·COCK AND THE·JEWEL.

Fable II.

The Cat and the Cock.

IT was the hard Fortune once of a *Cock*, to fall into the Clutches of a *Cat*. *Puss* had a Months Mind to be upon the Bones of him, but was not willing to pick a Quarrel however, without some plausible Colour for't. Sirrah (says she) what do you keep such a bawling, and screaming a Nights for, that no body can sleep near you? Alas says the *Cock*, I never wake any body, but when 'tis time for People to rise, and go about their Business. Come come, says *Puss*, without any more ado, 'tis time for me to go to Breakfast, and *Cats* don't live upon *Dialogues*; at which word she gave him a Pinch, and so made an end, both of the *Cock*, and of the *Story*.

The Moral.

'Tis an Easie Matter to find a Staff to Beat a Dog. *Innocence is no Protection against the Arbitrary Cruelty of a Tyrannical Power : But Reason and Conscience are yet so Sacred, that the Greatest Villanies are still Countenanc'd under that Cloak and Color.*

THE · CAT AND THE · COCK.

FABLE III.

The Wolf and the Lamb.

AS a *Wolf* was lapping at the Head of a Fountain, he spy'd a *Lamb*, paddling at the same time, a good way off down the Stream.   The *Wolf* had no sooner the Prey in his Eye, but away he runs open-mouth to't.   Villain (says he) how dare you lye muddling the Water that I'm a drinking?   Indeed, says the poor *Lamb*, I did not think that my drinking there *below*, could have foul'd your Water so far *above*.   Nay, says t'other, you'll never leave your chopping of Logick, till your Skin's turn'd over your Ears, as your Fathers was, a matter of six Months ago, for prating at this sawcy rate; you remember it full well, Sirrah.   If you'll believe me, Sir, (quoth the innocent *Lamb*, with fear and trembling) I was not come into the World then.   Why thou Impudence, cries the *Wolf*, hast thou neither Shame, nor Conscience?   But it runs in the Blood of your whole Race, Sirrah, to hate our Family; and therefore since Fortune has brought us together so conveniently, you shall e'en pay some of your Fore-Fathers Scores before you and I part; and so without any more ado, he leapt at the Throat of the miserable helpless *Lamb*, and tore him immediately to pieces.

The MORAL.

'Tis an Easie Matter to find a Staff to Beat a Dog.   *Innocence is no Protection against the Arbitrary Cruelty of a Tyrannical Power: But Reason and Conscience are yet so Sacred, that the Greatest Villanies are still Countenanc'd under that Cloak and Color.*

THE·WOLF AND THE·LAMB.

Fable IV.

The Kite, the Frog, and the Mouse.

THere fell out a Bloody Quarrel once betwixt the *Frogs* and the *Mice*, about the Sovereignty of the Fenns ; and whilst Two of their Champions were Disputing it at Swords Point, Down comes a *Kite* Powdering upon them in the *Interim*, and Gobbles up both together, to Part the Fray.

The MORAL.

'Tis the Fate of All Gotham Quarrels, *when Fools go together by the Ears, to have Knaves run away with the Stakes.*

THE·KITE·THE·FROG·AND·THE·MOUSE·

Fable V.

𝕿𝖍𝖊 𝕷𝖎𝖔𝖓, 𝖙𝖍𝖊 𝕭𝖊𝖆𝖗, 𝖆𝖓𝖉 𝖙𝖍𝖊 𝕱𝖔𝖝.

THere was a *Lion* and *Bear* had gotten a *Fawn* betwixt them, and there were they at it *Tooth and Nail*, which of the Two should carry't off. They Fought it out, till they were e'en glad to lie down, and take Breath. In which Instant, a *Fox* passing that way, and finding how the case stood with the Two Combatants, seized upon the *Fawn* for his Own Use, and so very fairly scamper'd away with him. The *Lion*, and the *Bear* saw the Whole Action, but not being in condition to Rise and Hinder it, they pass'd this Reflexion upon the whole matter; Here have we been Worrying one another, who should have the Booty, 'till this Cursed Fox has Bobb'd us Both on't.

The MORAL.

'Tis the Fate of All Gotham Quarrels, *when Fools go together by the Ears, to have Knaves run away with the Stakes.*

THE·LION;·THE·BEAR,·AND·THE·FOX.

Fable VI.

The Dog and the Shadow.

AS a *Dog* was crossing a River, with a Morsel of Good Flesh in his Mouth, he saw (as he thought) Another Dog under the Water, upon the very same Adventure. He never consider'd that the One was only the *Image* of the Other; but out of a Greediness to get Both, he Chops at the *Shadow*, and Loses the *Substance*.

The Moral.

All Covet, All Lose; *which may serve for a Reproof to Those that Govern their Lives by Fancy and Appetite, without Consulting the Honor, and the Justice of the Case.*

THE·DOG AND THE·SHADOW.

Fable VII.

The Wolf and the Crane.

A *Wolf* had got a Bone in's Throat, and could think of no better Instrument to Ease him of it, than the Bill of a *Crane ;* so he went and Treated with a *Crane* to help him out with it, upon Condition of a very considerable Reward for his pains. The *Crane* did him the Good Office, and then claim'd his Promise. Why how now Impudence! (says t'other) Do you put your Head into the Mouth of a *Wolf*, and then, when y'ave brought it out again safe and sound, do you talk of a Reward? Why Sirrah, you have your Head again, and is not that a Sufficient Recompence.

The Moral.

One Good Turn they say requires another : But yet He that has to do with Wild Beasts (as some Men are No Better) and comes off with a Whole Skin, let him Expect No Other Reward.

THE·WOLF AND THE·CRANE.

Fable VIII.

The Boar and the Ass.

AN *Ass* was so Hardy once, as to fall a Mopping and Braying at a *Boar*. The *Boar* began at first to shew his Teeth, and to Stomack the Affront; but upon Second Thoughts; Well! (says he) *Jeer on, and be an* Ass still. Take notice only by the way, that 'tis the Baseness of your Character that has sav'd your Carcass.

The Moral.

It is below the Dignity of a Great Mind to Entertain Contests with People that have neither Quality nor Courage: Beside the Folly of Contending with a Miserable Wretch, where the very Competition is a Scandal.

THE·BOAR AND THE·ASS.

FABLE IX.
The Country Mouse and the City Mouse.

THere goes an Old Story of a *Country Mouse* that Invited a *City-Sister* of hers to a Country Collation, where she spar'd for Nothing that the Place afforded; as Mouldy Crusts, Cheese-Parings, Musty Oatmeal, Rusty Bacon, and the like. Now the *City-Dame* was so well bred, as Seemingly to take All in Good Part : But yet at last, Sister (says she, after the Civilest Fashion) why will you be Miserable when you may be Happy ?   Why will you lie Pining, and Pinching yourself in such a Lonesome Starving Course of Life as This is ; when 'tis but going to Town along with Me ; to Enjoy all the Pleasures, and Plenty that Your Heart can Wish ?   This was a Temptation the *Country Mouse* was not able to Resist ; so that away they Trudg'd together, and about Midnight got to their Journeys End.   The *City-Mouse* show'd her Friend the Larder, the Pantry, the Kitchin, and Other Offices where she laid her Stores ; and after This, carry'd her into the Parlour, where they found, yet upon the Table, the Reliques of a Mighty Entertainment of That very Night.   The *City-Mouse* Carv'd her Companion of what she lik'd Best, and so to't they fell upon a Velvet Couch together : The Poor *Bumkin* that had never seen, nor heard of such Doings before, Bless'd herself at the Change of her Condition, when (as ill luck would have it) all on a Sudden, the Doors flew open, and in comes a Crew of Roaring Bullies, with their Wenches, their Dogs and their Bottles, and put the Poor *Mice* to their Wits End, how to save their Skins.   The Stranger Especially, that had never been at This Sport before ; but she made a Shift however for the present, to slink into a Corner, where she lay Trembling and Panting 'till the Company went their Way.   So soon as ever the House was Quiet again, Well : My *Court Sister*, says she, If This be the Way of Your *Town-Gamboles*, I'll e'en back to my Cottage, and my Mouldy Cheese again ; for I had much rather lie Knabbing of Crusts, without either Fear or Danger, in my Own Little Hole, than be Mistress of the Whole World with Perpetual Cares and Alarums.

The MORAL.

The Difference betwixt a Court and a Country Life. The Delights, Innocence, and Security of the One, Compar'd with the Anxiety, the Wickedness, and the Hazards of the Other.

THE·COUNTRY·MOUSE AND·THE·CITY·MOUSE·

Fable X.

The Crow and the Mussel.

THere was one of Your *Royston-Crows*, that lay Battering upon a *Mussel*, and could not for his Blood break the Shell to come at the Fish. A *Carrion-Crow*, in this *Interim*, comes up, and tells him, that what he could not do by Force, he might do by Stratagem. Take this *Mussel* up into the Air, says the *Crow*, as High as you can carry it, and then let him fall upon that Rock there; His Own Weight, You shall see, shall break him. The *Roystoner* took his Advice, and it succeeded accordingly; but while the One was upon Wing, the Other stood Lurching upon the Ground, and flew away with the Fish.

The Moral.

Charity begins at Home, *they say; and most People are kind to their Neighbours for their Own sakes.*

THE·CROW AND THE·MUSSEL·

Fable XI.

The Fox and the Crow.

A Certain *Fox* spy'd out a *Crow* upon a Tree with a Morsel in his mouth, that set his Chops a watering; but how to come at it was the Question. Oh thou Blessed Bird! (says he) the Delight of Gods, and of Men! and so he lays himself forth upon the Gracefulness of the *Crows* Person, and the Beauty of his Plumes; His Admirable Gift of *Augury*, &c., And now, says the *Fox*, If thou hadst but a Voice answerable to the rest of thy Excellent Qualities, the Sun in the Firmament could not shew the World such Another Creature. This Nauseous Flattery sets the *Crow* immediately a Gaping as Wide as ever he could stretch, to give the *Fox* a taste of his Pipe; but upon the Opening of his Mouth he drops his Breakfast, which the *Fox* presently Chopt up, and then bade him remember, that whatever he had said of his *Beauty*, he had spoken Nothing yet of his *Brains*.

The Moral.

There's hardly any man Living that may not be wrought upon more or less by Flattery: For we do all of us Naturally Overween in our Own Favour: But when it comes to be Apply'd once to a Vain Fool, it makes him forty times an Arranter Sot than he was before.

THE·FOX AND THE·CROW.

Fable XII.

The Old Lion.

A Lion that in the Days of his Youth and Strength, had been very Outragious and Cruel, came in the end to be Reduced by Old Age, and Infirmity, to the last Degree of Misery, and Contempt: Insomuch that All the Beasts of the Forest; some out of Insolence, others in Revenge, some in fine, upon One Pretence, some upon Another, fell upon him by Consent. He was a Miserable Creature to all Intents and Purposes; but Nothing went so near the Heart of him in his Distress, as to find himself Batter'd by the Heel of an *Ass*.

The Moral.

A Prince that does not secure Friends to Himself while he is in Power and Condition to oblige them, must never expect to find Friends, when he is Old and Impotent, and no longer Able to do them any Good. If he Governs Tyrannically in his Youth, he will be sure to be Treated Contemptuously in his Age; and the Baser his Enemies are, the more Insolent, and Intolerable will be the Affront.

THE·OLD·LION.

Fable XIII.

The Lion and the Mouse.

UPon the Roaring of a Beast in the Wood, a *Mouse* ran presently out to see what News: and what was it, but a *Lion*
Hamper'd in a Net! This Accident brought to her mind, how
that she herself, but some few Days before, had fall'n under the Paw
of a Certain Generous *Lion*, that let her go again. Upon a Strict
Enquiry into the Matter, she found This to be That very *Lion*;
and so set her self presently to Work upon the Couplings of the
Net; Gnaw'd the Threds to pieces, and in Gratitude Deliver'd her
Preserver.

The MORAL.

Without Good Nature, and Gratitude, Men had as good live in a
Wilderness as in a Society. There is no Subject so Inconsiderable, but
his Prince, at some time or Other, may have Occasion for him, and it
holds through the Whole Scale of the Creation, that the Great and the
Little have Need one of Another.

THE·LION AND THE·MOUSE.

Fable XIV.

The Sick Kite.

PRay *Mother* (says a Sick *Kite*) Give over these Idle Lamenta-tions, and let Me rather have your Prayers.   Alas! my Child, (says the Dam) which of the Gods shall I go to, for a Wretch that has Robb'd All their Altars?

The Moral.

Nothing but the Conscience of a Virtuous Life can make Death Easie to us; Wherefore there's No trusting to the Distraction of an Agonizing, and a Death-bed Repentance.

THE·SICK·KITE.

Fable XV.

The Swallow and other Birds.

THere was a Country Fellow at work a Sowing his Grounds, and a *Swallow* (being a Bird famous for Providence and Fore-sight) call'd a company of *Little Birds* about her, and bad 'em take Good Notice what that Fellow was a doing. You must know (says the *Swallow*) that all the Fowlers Nets and Snares are made of *Hemp*, or *Flax;* and that's the Seed that he is now a Sowing. Pick it up in time for fear of what may come on't. In short, they put it off, till it took Root; and then again, till it was sprung up into the Blade. Upon this, the *Swallow* told 'em once for All, that it was not yet too Late to prevent the Mischief, if they would but bestir themselves, and set Heartily about it; but finding that no Heed was given to what she said; She e'en bad adieu to her old Com-panions in the Woods, and so betook her self to a City Life, and to the Conversation of Men. This *Flax* and *Hemp* came in time to be gather'd, and Wrought, and it was this *Swallows* Fortune to see Several of the very same *Birds* that she had forewarn'd, taken in Nets, made of the very Stuff she told them off. They came at last to be Sensible of the folly of slipping their Opportunity; but they were Lost beyond All Redemption first.

The MORAL.

Wise Men read Effects in their Causes, but Fools will not Believe them till 'tis too late to prevent the Mischief. Delay in these Cases is Mortal.

THE SWALLOW AND OTHER BIRDS.

Fable XVI.
The Frogs Desiring a King.

IN the days of Old, when the *Frogs* were All at liberty in the Lakes, and grown quite Weary of living without Government, they Petition'd *Jupiter* for a *King*, to the End that there might be some Distinction of Good and Evil, by Certain Equitable Rules and Methods of Reward and Punishment. *Jupiter*, that knew the Vanity of their Hearts, threw them down a *Log* for their Governour; which, upon the first Dash, frighted the whole *Mobile* of them into the Mudd for the very fear on't. This *Panick* Terror kept them in Awe for a while, till in good time one *Frog*, Bolder than the Rest, put up his Head, and look'd about him, to see how squares went with their *New King*. Upon This, he calls his Fellow-Subjects together; Opens the truth of the Case; and Nothing would serve them then, but Riding a-top of him; Insomuch that the Dread they were in before, is now turn'd into Insolence, and Tumult. *This King*, they said, was too *Tame* for them, and *Jupiter* must needs be Entreated to send 'em Another: He did so, but Authors are Divided upon it, whether 'twas a *Stork*, or a *Serpent*; though whether of the Two soever it was, he left them neither Liberty, nor Property, but made a Prey of his Subjects. Such was their Condition in fine, that they sent *Mercury* to *Jupiter* yet once again for *Another King*, whose Answer was This: *They that will not be Contented when they are Well, must be Patient when Things are Amiss with them;* and People had better Rest where they are, than go farther, and fare Worse.

The Moral.

The Mobile *are Uneasie without a Ruler: They are as Restless with one; and the oftner they shift, the Worse they Are; So that Government, or No Government; a King of God's Making, or of the Peoples, or none at all; the Multitude are never to be satisfied.*

THE·FROGS·DESIRING·A·KING.

C

Fable XVII.

The Kite and the Pigeons.

THE *Pigeons* finding themselves Persecuted by the *Hawk*, made Choice of the *Kite* for their Guardian. The *Kite* sets up for their Protector, and is duly Crowned and Invested with Sovereign Rights; but under Countenance of That Authority, makes more Havock in the *Dove-House* in Two Days, than the *Hawk* could have done in Twice as many Months.

The Moral.

Tis a Dangerous Thing for People to call in a Powerful and an Ambitious man for their Protector; and upon the Clamour of here and there a Private person, to hazard the Whole Community.

THE·KITE AND THE·PIGEONS.

Fable XVIII.

The Sow and the Wolf.

A Wolf came to a Sow that was just preparing to lye down, and very kindly offer'd to take care of her Litter. The Sow as Civily thank'd her for her Love, and desir'd she would be pleas'd to stand off a little, and do her the Good Office at a Distance.

The Moral.

There are no Snares so Dangerous as those that are laid for us under the Name of Good Offices.

THE·SOW AND THE·WOLF.

Fable XIX.

The Old Dog and his Master.

AN *Old Dog*, that in his Youth had led his *Master* many a Merry Chase, and done him all the Offices of a Trusty Servant, came at last, upon falling from his Speed and Vigor, to be Loaden at every turn with Blows and Reproaches for it. Why Sir, (says the *Dog*) My Will is as Good as ever it was ; but my Strength, and my Teeth are gone ; and you might with as good a Grace, and Every jot as much Justice, Hang me up because I'm *Old*, as Beat me because I'm *Impotent*.

The Moral.

The Reward of Affection and Fidelity must be the Work of another World ; Not but that the Conscience of Well Doing is a Comfort that may pass for a Recompence even in This ; in Despite of Ingratitude and Injustice

THE·OLD·DOG AND·HIS MASTER.

Fable XX.

The Hares and the Frogs.

ONce upon a time the *Hares* found themselves mightily Un-satisfy'd with the Miserable Condition they Liv'd in, and call'd a Council to Advise upon't. Here we live, says one of 'em, at the Mercy of Men, Dogs, Eagles, and I know not how many Other Creatures and Vermin, that Prey upon us at Pleasure; Perpetually in Frights, Perpetually in Danger; And therefore I am absolutely of Opinion that we had Better Die once for All, than live at This rate in a Continual Dread that's Worse than Death it self. The Motion was Seconded and Debated, and a Resolution Immediately taken, *One and All*, to Drown Themselves. The Vote was no sooner pass'd, but away they Scudded with That Determination to the Next River. Upon this Hurry, there leapt a Whole Shoal of *Frogs* from the Bank into the Water, for fear of the *Hares*. Nay, then my Masters, says one of the Gravest of the Company, pray let's have a little Patience. Our Condition I find is not altogether so bad as we fancy'd it; for there are Those you see that are as much affraid of Us, as we are of Others.

The Moral.

There's No Contending with the Orders and Decrees of Providence. He that Made us knowes what's Fittest for us; and Every man's Own Lot (well Understood and Manag'd) is Undoubtedly the Best.

THE·HARES·AND·FROGS·

Fable XXI.

𝕿𝖍𝖊 𝕯𝖔𝖌 𝖆𝖓𝖉 𝖙𝖍𝖊 𝕾𝖍𝖊𝖊𝖕.

A *Dog* brought an Action, before the *Wolf* and the *Kite* as Judges, of the Case against a *Sheep*, for some Certain Measures of Wheat, that he had lent him.   The *Plaintiff* prov'd the Debt. The *Defendent* was cast in *Costs and Damages*, and forc'd to sell the Wool off his Back to Satisfie the Creditor.

The Moral.

'Tis not a Straw matter whether the Main Cause be Right or Wrong, or the Charge True or False; Where the Bench, and Jury are in a Conspiracy against the Pris'ner.

THE DOG AND THE SHEEP.

Fable XXII.

The Fox and the Stork.

THere was a Great Friendship once betwixt a *Fox* and a *Stork*, and the Former would needs Invite the Other to a Treat. They had Several Soups serv'd up in Broad Dishes and Plates, and so the *Fox* fell to Lapping Himself, and bad his Guest Heartily Welcom to what was before him. The *Stork* found he was Put upon, but set so good a Face however upon his Entertainment; that his Friend by All means must take a Supper with Him That night in Revenge. The *Fox* made Several Excuses upon the Matter of Trouble and Expence, but the *Stork* in fine, would not be said Nay; So that at last, he promis'd him to come. The Collation was serv'd up in Glasses, with Long Narrow Necks, and the Best of Every thing that was to be had. Come (says the *Stork* to his Friend) Pray be as Free as if you were at home, and so fell to't very Savourly Himself. The *Fox* quickly found This to be a Trick, though he could not but Allow of the Contrivance as well as the Justice of the Revenge. For such a Glass of Sweet-Meats to the One, was just as much to the Purpose, as a Plate of Porridge to the Other.

The MORAL.

'Tis allowable in all the Liberties of Conversation to give a Man a Rowland *for his* Oliver, *and to* pay *him in his Own Coin, as we say; provided always that we keep within the Compass of Honour, and Good Manners.*

THE FOX AND THE STORK.

Fable XXIII.

The Fox and the Mask.

AS a *Fox* was Rummidging among a Great many *Masks*, there was One very Extraordinary one among the Rest. He took it up, and when he had Considered it a while, Well, (says he) What Pity 'tis, that so Exquisite an Outside of a Head should not have one Grain of Sense in't.

The MORAL.

'Tis not the Barber or the Taylor that makes the Man; and 'tis No New Thing to see a Fine Wrought Head without so much as One Grain of Salt in't.

THE·FOX AND THE·MASK.

Fable XXIV.

The Jackdaw and the Peacocks.

A *Jackdaw* that had a mind to be Sparkish, Trick'd himself up with all the *Gay-Feathers* he could Muster together: And upon the Credit of these Stoll'n, or Borrow'd Ornaments, he Valu'd himself above All the Birds in the Air Beside. The Pride of this Vanity got him the Envy of all his Companions, who, upon a Discovery of the Truth of the Case, fell to Pluming of him by Consent; and when Every Bird had taken his Own *Feather*; the Silly *Jackdaw* had Nothing left him to Cover his Nakedness.

The MORAL.

We steal from one Another all manner of Ways, and to all manner of Purposes; Wit, as well as Feathers; but where Pride and Beggery Meet, people are sure to be made Ridiculous in the Conclusion.

THE JACKDAW AND THE PEACOCKS.

D

FABLE XXV.

The Ox and the Frog.

AS a Huge Over-grown *Ox* was Grazing in a Meadow, an Old Envious *Frog* that stood Gaping at him hard by, call'd out to her Little Ones, to take Notice of the Bulk of That Monstrous Beast ; and see, says she, if I don't make my self now the Bigger of the Two.   So she Strain'd Once, and Twice, and went still swelling on and on, till in the Conclusion she Forc'd her self, and Burst.

The MORAL.

Betwixt Pride, Envy, and Ambition, men fancy Themselves to be Bigger than they are, and Other People to be Less : And This Tumour Swells itself at last 'till it makes All Fly.

THE·OX AND THE·FROG.

Fable XXVI.

The Horse and the Lion.

THere was an Old Hungry *Lion* would fain have been Dealing with a piece of Good *Horse-Flesh* that he had in his Eye; but the *Nag* he thought would be too Fleet for him, unless he could Supply the want of Heels, by Artifice and Address. He Imitates the Ways and Habits of a Professor of Physick, and according to the Humor of the World, sets up for a Doctor of the College. Under this Pretext, he lets fall a Word or two by way of Discourse, upon the Subject of his Trade ; but the *Horse* Smelt him out, and presently a Crotchet came in his Head how he might Countermine him. I got a Thorn in my Foot T'other day, says the *Horse*, as I was Crossing a Thicket, and I am e'en quite Lame on't. Oh, says the New Physician, Do but hold up your Leg a little, and I'll Cure ye immediately. The *Lion* presently puts himself in posture for the Office ; but the Patient was too Nimble for his Doctor, and so soon as ever he had him Fair for his Purpose, gave him so Terrible a Rebuke upon the Forehead with his Heel, that he laid him at his Length, and so got off with a whole Skin, before the Other could Execute his Design.

The MORAL.

Harm Watch, Harm Catch, *is but according to the Common Rule of Equity and Retaliation, and a very Warrantable Way of Deceiving the Deceiver.*

THE·HORSE AND THE·LION.

FABLE XXVII.

The Horse and the Ass.

IN the Days of Old, when *Horses* spoke *Greek* and *Latin*, and *Asses* made *Syllogisms*, there happen'd an Encounter upon the Road, betwixt a Proud Pamper'd *Jade* in the Full Course of his Carriere, and a Poor Creeping *Ass*, under a Heavy Burden, that had Chopt into the same Track with him. Why, how now Sirrah, says he, D'ye not see by these Arms, and Trappings, to what Master I belong? And D'ye not Understand that when I have That Master of mine upon my Back, the Whole Weight of the State rests upon My Shoulders? Out of the way thou slavish Insolent Animal, or I'll Tread thee to Dirt. The Wretched *Ass* immediately Slunk aside, with this Envious Reflection between his Teeth. [*What would I give to Change Conditions with That Happy Creature there.*] This Fancy would not out of the Head of him, 'till it was his Hap some Few Days after to see This very *Horse* doing Drudgery in a Common Dung-Cart. Why how now Friend (says the *Ass*) How comes This about? Only the Chance of the War, says the Other: I was a *Soldiers Horse*, you must know; and my Master carry'd me into a Battle, where I was Shot, Hack'd, and Maim'd; and you have here before Your Eyes the Catastrophe of My Fortune.

The MORAL.

The Folly, and the Fate, of Pride and Arrogance. The Mistake of Placing Happiness in any thing that may be taken away, and the Blessing of Freedom in a Mean Estate.

THE·HORSE AND THE·ASS.

Fable XXVIII.

The Birds, the Beasts, and the Bat.

UPon a Desperate and a Doubtful Battel betwixt the *Birds* and the *Beasts*, the *Bat* stood *Neuter*, till she found that the *Beasts* had the Better on't, and then went over to the Stronger Side. But it came to pass afterward (as the Chance of War is Various) that the *Birds* Rally'd their Broken Troops, and carry'd the Day; and away she went Then to T'other Party, where she was Try'd by a Council of War as a Deserter; Stript, Banish'd, and finally Condemn'd never to see Day-light again.

The MORAL.

Trimming *in some Cases, is Foul, and Dishonest; in others Laudable, and in some again, not only Honest, but Necessary. The Nicety lies in the skill of Distinguishing upon Cases, Times, and Degrees.*

THE·BIRDS·THE·BEASTS AND THE·BAT.

Fable XXIX.

The Fox and the Wolf.

A *Wolf* that had a mind to take his Ease, Stor'd himself Privately with Provisions, and so kept Close awhile. Why, how now Friend, says a *Fox* to him, we han't seen You abroad at the Chace this many a day! Why truly says the *Wolf*, I have gotten an Indisposition that keeps me much at Home, and I hope I shall have Your Prayers for my Recovery. The *Fox* had a Fetch in't, and when he saw it would not Fadge; Away goes he presently to a Shepherd, and tells him where he might surprize a *Wolf* if he had a mind to't. The Shepherd follow'd his Directions, and Destroy'd him. The *Fox* immediately, as his Next Heir, repairs to his Cell, and takes possession of his Stores: but he had Little Joy of the Purchase, for in a very short time, the same Shepherd did as much for the *Fox*, as he had done before for the *Wolf*.

The Moral.

'*Tis with* Sharpers *as 'tis with* Pikes, *they Prey upon their own kind; And 'tis a Pleasant Scene enough, when Thieves fall out among themselves, to see the Cutting of One Diamond with Another*

THE·FOX AND THE·WOLF.

FABLE XXX.

The Stag Looking into the Water.

AS a *Stag* was Drinking upon the Bank of a Clear Stream, he saw his Image in the Water, and Enter'd into This Contemplation upon't. Well! says he, if These Pityful Shanks of mine were but Answerable to this Branching Head, I can but think how I should Defy all my Enemies. The Words were hardly out of his Mouth, but he Discovered a Pack of Dogs coming full-Cry towards him. Away he Scours cross the Fields, Casts off the Dogs, and Gains a Wood; but Pressing through a Thicket, the Bushes held him by the Horns, till the Hounds came in, and Pluck'd him Down. The Last Thing he said was This. What an Unhappy Fool was I, to Take my Friends for my Enemies, and my Enemies for my Friends! I trusted to my *Head*, that has Betray'd me, and I found fault with my *Legs*, that would otherwise have brought me off.

The MORAL.

He that does not thoroughly know himself, may be well allowed to make a False Judgment upon other Matters that most Nearly concern him.

THE·STAG LOOKING·INTO THE·WATER

Fable XXXI.

The Snake and the File.

THere was a *Snake* got into a Smith's Shop, and fell to Licking of a *File*. She Saw the *File* Bloody, and still the Bloodier it was, the more Eagerly she Lick'd it; upon a Foolish Fancy, that it was the *File* that Bled, and that She her self had the Better on't. In the Conclusion, when she could Lick no Longer, she fell to Biting; but finding at last she could do no more Good upon't with her Teeth than with her Tongue, she Fairly left it.

The MORAL.

'Tis a Madness to stand Biting and Snapping at any thing to no manner of purpose, more than the Gratifying of an Impotent Rage, in the fancy of Hurting Another, when in truth, we only Wound our selves.

THE·SNAKE AND THE·FILE.

Fable XXXII.
The Wolves and the Sheep.

THere was a Time when the *Sheep* were so Hardy as to Wage War with the *Wolves*; and so long as they had the *Dogs* for their Allies, they were upon all Encounters, at least a Match for their Enemies. Upon This Consideration, the *Wolves* sent their Embassadors to the *Sheep*, to Treat about a Peace, and in the Mean Time there were Hostages given on Both Sides; the *Dogs* on the part of the *Sheep*, and the *Wolves Whelps* on the Other Part, 'till Matters might be brought to an Issue. While they were upon Treaty, the *Whelps* fell a Howling; The *Wolves* cryed out Treason; and pretending an Infraction in the Abuse of their Hostages, fell upon the *Sheep* immediately without their *Dogs*, and made them pay for the Improvidence of leaving themselves without a Guard.

The Moral.

'Tis senseless to the Highest Degree to think of Establishing an Alliance among those that Nature her self has Divided, by an Inconciliable Disagreement. Beside, that a Foolish Peace is much more Destructive than a Bloody War.

THE·WOLVES AND THE·SHEEP.

E

Fable XXXIII.

The Ape and the Fox.

AN *Ape* that found Many Inconveniences by going *Tail-less*, went to a *Fox* that had a Well-spread, Bushy *Tail*, and begg'd of him only a little piece on't to Cover his Nakedness: For (says he) you have enough for Both, and what needs more than you have Occasion for? Well, *John* (says the *Fox*) be it More, or be it Less, you get not one single Hair on't; for I would have ye know, Sirrah, that the *Tail* of a *Fox* was never made for the Buttocks of an *Ape*.

The MORAL.

Providence has Assign'd Every Creature its Station, Lot, Make and Figure; and 'tis not for Us to stand Correcting the Works of an Incomprehensible Wisdom, and an Almighty Power.

THE·APE·AND·THE·FOX·

Fable XXXIV.

The Lark and her Young Ones.

THere was a Brood of Young *Larks* in the Corn, and the *Dam*, when she went abroad to Forrage for them, laid a Strict Charge upon her *Little Ones*, to pick up what News they could get against she came back again. They told her at her Return, that the Owner of the Field had been there, and Order'd his Neighbours to come and Reap the Corn. Well, says the *Old One*, there's no Danger yet then. They told her the next Day that he had been there again, and Desir'd his Friends to Do't. Well, well, says she, there's no Hurt in That neither, and so she went out Progging for Provisions again as before. But upon the Third Day, when they told their Mother, that the Master and his Son appointed to come Next Morning and do't Themselves: Nay then, says she, 'tis time to look about us: As for the Neighbours and the Friends, I fear 'em not; but the Master I'm sure will be as good as his Word; for 'tis his own Business.

The Moral.

He that would be sure to have his Bus'ness Well Done, must either Do it Himself, or see the Doing of it; Beside that many a Good Servant is Spoil'd by a Careless Master.

THE·LARK AND ·HER YOUNG·ONES.

Fable XXXV.

The Stag in the Ox-Stall.

A *Stag* that was hard set by the Huntsmen, betook himself to a Stall for Sanctuary, and prevail'd with the *Oxen* to Conceal him the Best they could, so they cover'd him with Straw, and by and by in comes the Keeper to Dress the Cattel, and to Feed them ; and when he had done his Work he went his Way without any Discovery. The *Stag* reckon'd himself by This Time to be out of all Danger; but One of the *Oxen* that had more Brains than his Fellows, advis'd him not to be too Confident neither; for the Servant, says he, is a Puzzling Fool, that heeds Nothing ; but when my Master comes, he'll have an Eye *Here and There and Every where*, and will most certainly find ye out. Upon the very Speaking of the Word, in comes the Master, and He spies out Twenty Faults, I warrant ye; This was not Well, and That was not Well; till at last, as he was Prying and Groping up and down, he felt the Horns of the *Stag* under the Straw, and so made Prize of him.

The Moral.

He that would be sure to have his Bus'ness Well Done, must either Do it Himself, or see the Doing of it ; Beside that many a Good Servant is Spoil'd by a Careless Master.

THE·STAG·IN·THE·OX-STALL.

Fable XXXVI.
The Fox and the Sick Lion.

A Certain *Lion* that had got a Politique Fit of Sickness, made it his Observation, that of All the Beasts in the Forest, the *Fox* never came at him: And so he wrote him Word how Ill he was, and how Mighty Glad he should be of his Company, upon the Score of Ancient Friendship and Acquaintance. The *Fox* return'd the Complement with a Thousand Prayers for his Recovery; but as for Waiting upon him, he desir'd to be Excus'd; For (says he) I find the Traces of abundance of Feet Going In to Your Majesty's Palace, and not One that comes Back again.

The Moral.

The Kindnesses of Ill Natur'd and Designing People, should be thoroughly Consider'd, and Examin'd, before we give Credit to them.

THE·FOX AND THE·SICK·LION.

Fable XXXVII.

The Stag and the Horse.

UPon a Dispute betwixt a *Stag* and a *Horse* about a piece of Pasture, the *Stag* got the Better on't, and beat the Other out of the Field. The *Horse*, upon This Affront, Advis'd with a *Man* what Course to Take; who told him, that if he would Submit to be Bridled, and Sadled, and take a *Man* upon his Back with a Lance in his Hand, he would undertake to give him the Satisfaction of a Revenge. The *Horse* came to his Terms, and for the Gratifying of a Present Passion, made himself a Slave all the days of his Life. *Stesichorus* made use of This Fable, to Divert the *Himerenses* from Chusing *Phalaris* the Tyrant for their General. This *Horse's* Case, says he, will be Yours, if you go on with your Proposals. 'Tis true, You'l have your *Revenge*, but you'l lose your *Liberties*; Upon which Words the Motion fell.

The Moral.

Let every Man take a True Measure of Himself, what he is Able to do, and what Not; before he comes to any Peremptory Resolution how to Proceed. He is a Madman, that to Avoid a Present, and a Less Evil, runs Blindfold into a Greater; and for the Gratifying of a Froward Humour, makes himself a Slave All the Days of his Life.

THE·STAG AND THE·HORSE.

Fable XXXVIII.

The Horse and the Loaded Ass.

AS a *Horse* and an *Ass* were upon the Way together, the *Ass* cryed out to his Companion, to Ease him of his Burden, though never so little, he should fall down Dead else. The *Horse* would not; and so his Fellow-Servant sunk under his Load. The Master, upon This, had the *Ass* Flay'd, and laid his Whole Pack, Skin and All, upon the *Horse*. Well, (says he) This Judgment is befall'n me for my Ill Nature, in refusing to help my Brother in the Depth of his Distress.

The Moral.

It is a Christian, a Natural, a Reasonable, and a Political Duty, for All Members of the same Body to Assist One Another.

THE·HORSE AND THE·LOADED·ASS

FABLE XXXIX.
The Dog and the Wolf.

THere was a Hagged Carrion of a *Wolf*, and a Jolly Sort of a Gentile *Dog*, with Good Flesh upon's Back, that fell into Company together upon the King's High-Way. The *Wolf* was wonderfully pleas'd with his Companion, and as Inquisitive to Learn how he brought himself to That Blessed State of Body. Why, says the *Dog*, I keep my Master's House from Thieves, and I have very Good Meat, Drink, and Lodging for my pains. Now if you'll go along with Me, and do as I do, you may fare as I fare. The *Wolf* Struck up the Bargain, and so away they Trotted together: But as they were Jogging on, the *Wolf* spy'd a Bare Place about the *Dog's* Neck, where the Hair was worn off. Brother (says he) how comes this I prethee? Oh, That's Nothing, says the *Dog*, but the Fretting of my *Collar* a little. Nay, says T'other, if there be a *Collar* in the Case, I know Better Things than to sell my Liberty for a Crust.

The MORAL.

We are so Dazzl'd with the Glare of a Splendid Appearance, that we can hardly Discern the Inconveniencies that Attend it. 'Tis a Comfort to have Good Meat and Drink at Command, and Warm Lodging: But He that sells his Freedom for the Cramming of his Belly, has but a Hard Bargain of it.

THE·DOG AND THE·WOLF.

Fable XL.

𝕿𝖍𝖊 𝕱𝖔𝖝 𝖆𝖓𝖉 𝖙𝖍𝖊 𝕷𝖎𝖔𝖓.

A *Fox* had the hap to fall into the Walk of a *Lion;* (the First of the Kind that ever he saw) and he was ready to Drop down at the very sight of him. He came a While after, to see Another, and was Frighted still; but Nothing to What he was Before. It was his Chance, after This, to Meet a Third *Lion;* and he had the Courage, Then, to Accost him, and to make a kind of Acquaintance with him.

The Moral.

Novelty Surprizes us, and we have Naturally a Horrour for Uncouth Misshapen Monsters; but 'tis our Ignorance that staggers us, for upon Custom and Experience, All These Bugs grow Familiar, and Easy to us.

THE FOX AND THE LION

FABLE XLI.

The Eagle and the Fox.

THere was a Bargain struck up betwixt an *Eagle* and a *Fox*, to be Wonderful Good Neighbours and Friends. The One Took Up in a Thicket of Brushwood, and the Other Timber'd upon a Tree hard by. The *Eagle*, One Day when the *Fox* was abroad a Forraging, fell into his Quarters and carry'd away a Whole Litter of Cubs at a Swoop. The *Fox* came time enough back to see the *Eagle* upon Wing, with her Prey in the Foot, and to send many a Heavy Curse after her; but there was No overtaking her: It happen'd in a very Short time after This, upon the Sacrificing of a *Goat*, that the same *Eagle* made a Stoop at a piece of Flesh upon the Altar, and she took it away to her Young: But some Live-Coales it seems, that Stuck to't, set the Nest a fire. The Birds were not as yet Fledg'd enough to Shift for Themselves, but upon Sprawling and Struggling to get Clear of the Flame, down they Tumbled, half Roasted into the very Mouth of the *Fox*, that stood Gaping under the Tree to see the End on't: So that the *Fox* had the Satisfaction at last, of Devouring the Children of her Enemy in the very Sight of the Dam.

The MORAL.

God Reserves to Himself the Punishment of Faithless, and Oppressing Governours, and the Vindication of his Own Worship and Altars.

THE·EAGLE AND THE·FOX.

Fable XLII.

The Husbandman and the Stork.

A Poor Innocent *Stork* had the Ill Hap to be taken in a Net that was layd for *Geese* and *Cranes*. The *Storks* Plea for her self was Simplicity, and Piety : The Love she bore to Mankind, and the Service she did in Picking up of Venemous Creatures. This is all True, says the *Husbandman* ; But They that Keep Ill Company, if they be Catch'd with Ill Company, must Expect to suffer with Ill Company.

The Moral.

'Tis as much as a man's Life, Fortune, and Reputation, are Worth to keep Good Company (over and above the Contagion of Lewd Examples) for as Birds of a Feather will Flock together, *so if the Good and the Bad be taken together, they must Expect to go the Way of All Flesh together.*

A HARMLESS STORK

THE·HUSBANDMAN AND·THE STORK·

Fable XLIII.
The Shepherd's Boy.

A *Shepherd's Boy* had gotten a Roguy Trick of crying [a *Wolf*, a *Wolf*] when there was no such Matter, and Fooling the Country People with *False Alarms*. He had been at This Sport so many times in Jest, that they would not Believe him at last when he was in Earnest : And so the *Wolves* Brake in upon the Flock, and Worry'd the *Sheep* at Pleasure.

The Moral.

He must be a very Wise Man that knows the True Bounds, and Measures of Fooling, with a respect to Time, Place, Matters, Persons, &c. But Religion, Business and Cases of Consequence must be Excepted out of That sort of Liberty.

THE SHEPHERD'S BOY.

Fable XLIV.

The Eagle and the Crow.

AN *Eagle* made a Stoop at a *Lamb*; Truss'd it, and took it Cleverly away with her. A Mimical *Crow*, that saw This Exploit, would needs try the same Experiment upon a Ram: But his Claws were so Shackled in the Fleece with Lugging to get him up, that the Shepherd came in, and Caught him, before he could Clear Himself; He Clipt his Wings, and carried him Home to his Children to Play withal. They came Gaping about him, and ask'd their Father what Strange Bird that Was? Why, says he, He'll tell you Himself that he's an *Eagle*; but if you'll take My Word for't; I know him to be a *Crow*.

The Moral.

'Tis a High Degree of Vanity and Folly, for Men to take More upon them than they are able to go through withall; And the End of Those Undertakings is only Mockery and Disappointment in the Conclusion.

THE·EAGLE AND THE·CROW.

Fable XLV.

The Dog in the Manger.

A Churlish Envious *Cur* was gotten into a *Manger*, and there lay Growling and Snarling to keep the Horses from their Provender. The *Dog* Eat None himself, and yet rather Ventur'd the Starving his Own Carcase than he would suffer any thing else to be the Better for't.

The Moral.

Envy pretends to No Other Happiness than what it derives from the Misery of Other People, and will rather Eat Nothing it self than not Starve Those that Would.

THE·DOG·IN·THE·MANGER.

Fable XLVI.

Jupiter and the Camel.

IT stuck filthily in the Camel's Stomach, that *Bulls*, *Stags*, *Lions*, *Bears*, and the like, should be Armed with *Horns*, *Teeth*, and *Claws*, and that a Creature of his Size should be left Naked and Defenceless. Upon This Thought he fell down upon his Marrowbones, and begg'd of *Jupiter* to give him a pair of Horns, but the Request was so Ridiculous, that *Jupiter*, instead of *Horning* him, Order'd him to be Cropt, and so Punish'd him with the loss of his *Ears* which Nature had Allow'd him, for being so Unreasonable as to Ask for *Horns*, that Providence never intended him.

The MORAL.

The Bounties of Heaven are in such manner Distributed, that Every Living Creature has its Share; beside, that to Desire Things against Nature, is Effectually to Blame the very Author of Nature it self.

JUPITER AND THE·CAMEL·

FABLE XLVII.

The fox and the hare to Jupiter.

A *Fox* and a *Hare* Presented a Petition to *Jupiter*. The *Fox* pray'd for the *Hare's* Swiftness of Foot, and the *Hare* for the *Fox's* Craft, and Wyliness of Address. *Jupiter* told them, that since every Creature had some Advantage or Other Peculiar to it self, it would not stand with Divine Justice, that had provided so well for Every One in Particular, to Confer All upon any One.

The MORAL.

The Bounties of Heaven are in such manner Distributed, that Every Living Creature has its Share; beside, that to Desire Things against Nature, is Effectually to Blame the very Author of Nature it self.

THE·FOX AND THE·HARE TO·JUPITER·

Fable XLVIII.
The Peacock's Complaint.

THE *Peacock*, they say, laid it Extremely to Heart, that being *Juno's Darling-Bird*, he had not the *Nightingale's* Voice super-added to the Beauty of his own Plumes. Upon This Subject he Petition'd his Patroness, who gave him for Answer, that Providence had Assigned Every Bird its Proportion, and so bad him Content himself with his Lot.

The MORAL.

The Bounties of Heaven are in such manner Distributed, that Every Living Creature has its Share ; beside, that to Desire Things against Nature, is Effectually to Blame the very Author of Nature it self.

THE ❀ PEACOCK'S ❀ COMPLAINT.

G

FABLE XLIX.

The Fox and the Goat.

A *Fox* and a *Goat* went down by Consent into a Well to Drink, and when they had Quench'd their Thirst, the *Goat* fell to Hunting up and down which way to get back again. Oh! says *Reynard*, Never Trouble your Head how to get back, but leave That to Me. Do but You Raise your self upon your Hinder Legs with your Fore-Feet Close to the Wall, and then stretch out your Head: I can Easily Whip up to your Horns, and so out of the Well, and Draw you after me. The *Goat* puts himself in a Posture immediately as he was directed, gives the *Fox* a Lift, and so Out he Springs; but *Reynard's* Bus'ness was now only to make Sport with his Companion instead of Helping Him. Some Hard Words the *Goat* gave him, but the *Fox* puts off all with a Jest. If you had but half so much Brain as Beard, says he, you would have bethought your self how to get up again before you went down.

The MORAL.

A Wise Man will Debate Every Thing Pro *and* Con *before he comes to Fix upon any Resolution. He leaves Nothing to Chance more than Needs must. There must be No Bantering out of Season.*

THE·FOX AND THE·GOAT.

Fable L.

The Partridge and the Cocks.

A *Cock-Master* bought a *Partridge*, and turn'd it among his *Fighting Cocks*, for them to feed together. The *Cocks* beat the *Partridge* away from their Meat, which she lay'd the more to Heart, because it look'd like an Aversion to her purely as a Stranger. But the *Partridge* finding These very *Cocks* afterwards, Cutting one Another to pieces, she comforted herself with This Thought, that she had no Reason to expect they should be Kinder to Her, than they were to One Another.

The Moral.

'Tis No Wonder to find Those People Troublesome to Strangers, that Cannot Agree among Themselves. They Quarrel for the Love of Quarrelling ; and provided the Peace be broken, No matter upon What Ground, or with Whom.

THE·PARTRIDGE AND THE·COCKS.

Fable LI.

The Tunny and the Dolphin.

A *Tunny* gave Chace to a *Dolphin*; and when he was just ready to seize him, the *Tunny* struck before he was aware, and the *Dolphin*, in the Eagerness of his Pursuit, ran himself a ground with him. They were both Lost; but the *Tunny* kept his Eye still upon the *Dolphin*, and Observing him when he was Just at Last Gasp: Well, says he, the Thought of Death is now Easy to me, so long as I see my Enemy go for Company.

The Moral.

'Tis a Wretched Satisfaction, that a Revengeful Man takes, even in the Losing of his own Life, provided that his Enemy may go for Company.

THE·TUNNY AND THE·DOLPHIN.

Fable LII.

The Fox without a Tail.

THere was a *Fox* taken in a Trap, that was glad to Compound for his Neck by leaving his *Tail* behind him. It was so Uncouth a Sight, for a *Fox* to appear without a *Tail*, that the very Thought on't made him e'en Weary of his Life; for 'twas a Loss never to be Repair'd : But however for the Better Countenance of the Scandal, he got *the Master and Wardens of the Foxes Company* to call a *Court of Assistants*, where he himself appeared, and made a Learned Discourse upon the Trouble, the Uselessness, and the Indecency of *Foxes* Wearing *Tails*. He had no sooner say'd out his Say, but up rises a Cunning Snap, then at the Board, who desir'd to be Inform'd, whether the Worthy Member that Mov'd against the Wearing of *Tails* gave his Advice for the Advantage of Those that *Had Tails*, or to Palliate the Deformity and Disgrace of Those that had *None*.

The MORAL.

When a Man has any Notable Defect, or Infirmity about him, whether by Nature, or by Chance, 'tis the Best of his Play, to try the humour, if he can turn it into a Fashion.

THE·FOX·WITHOUT·A·TAIL.

Fable LIII.

The Fox and the Bramble.

A *Fox* that was close Pursu'd, took a Hedge, The Bushes gave way, and in Catching hold of a *Bramble* to break his Fall, the Prickles ran into his Feet. Upon This, He layd himself down, and fell to Licking his Paws, with Bitter Exclamations against the *Bramble*. Good Words, *Reynard*, says the *Bramble*, One would have thought you had known Better Things, than to Expect a Kindness from a Common Enemy, and to lay hold on That for Relief, that Catches at Every Thing else for Mischief.

The Moral.

There are some Malicious Natures that Place all their Delight in doing Ill Turns, and That Man is hard put to't that is first brought into a Distress, and then forc'd to Fly to such People for Relief.

THE·FOX AND THE·BRAMBLE·

Fable LIV.

The Fox and the Crocodile.

THere happen'd a Contest betwixt a *Fox* and a *Crocodile*, upon the Point of Blood and Extraction. The *Crocodile* Amplify'd Wonderfully upon his Family, for the Credit of his Ancestors. Friend (says the *Fox*, smiling upon't) there will need no Herald to Prove your Gentility ; for you carry the Marks of Your Original in Your very Skin.

The Moral.

Great Boasters and Lyars have the Fortune still some way or other to Disprove themselves.

.THE·FOX AND·THE CROCODILE.

Fable LV.

The Boasting Mule.

THere was a *Favourite-Mule*, that was High Fed, and in the Pride of Flesh and Mettle, would still be Bragging of his Family, and his Ancestors. My Father (says he) was a Coarser, and though I say it that should not say't, I my self take after him. He had no sooner spoke the Words, but he was put to the Tryal of his Heels, and did not only shew himself a Jade; but in the very Heat of his Ostentation, his Father fell a Braying, which Minded him of his Original, and the Whole Field made Sport on't, when they found him to be the Son of an *Ass*.

The MORAL.

A Bragging Fool that's Rais'd out of a Dunghill, and sets up for a Man of Quality, is Asham'd of Nothing in This World but of his Own Father.

THE·BOASTING·MULE.

Fable LVI.

The Lion in Love.

A *Lion* fell in Love with a Country Lass, and desir'd her Father's Consent to have her in Marriage. The Answer he gave was Churlish enough. He'd never Agree to't he said, upon any Terms, to Marry his Daughter to a Beast. The *Lion* gave him a Sour Look upon't, which brought the Bumkin, upon Second Thoughts, to strike up a Bargain with him, upon these Conditions; that his Teeth should be Drawn, and his Nails Par'd; for Those were Things, he said, that the Foolish Girl was Terribly afraid of. The *Lion* sends for a Surgeon immediately to do the Work; (as what will not Love make a Body do?) And so soon as ever the Operation was Over, he goes and Challenges the Father upon his Promise. The Countryman seeing the *Lion* Disarm'd, Pluck'd up a Good Heart, and with a Swinging Cudgel so Order'd the Matter, that he broke off the Match.

The Moral.

An Extravagant Love consults neither Life, Fortune, nor Reputation, but Sacrifices All that can be Dear to a Man of Sense and Honour, to the Transports of an Inconsiderate Passion.

THE·LION·IN·LOVE

FABLE LVII.

The Lioness and the Fox.

A Numerous Issue passes in the World for a Blessing; and This Consideration made a *Fox* cast it in the Teeth of a *Lioness*, that she brought forth but One Whelp at a time. Very Right, says the Other, but then That *One* is a *Lion*.

The MORAL.

'*Tis a Common Thing to Value things more by the Number, than by the Excellency of them.*

THE·LIONESS AND THE·FOX.

Fable LVIII.

The Fighting Cocks and the Eagle.

TWO *Cocks* fought a Duel for the Mastery of a Dunghil. He that was Worsted, slunk away into a Corner, and Hid himself; T'other takes his Flight up to the Top of the House, and there with Crowing and Clapping of his Wings makes Proclamation of his Victory. An *Eagle* made a Stoop at him in the Middle of his Exultation, and carry'd him away. By This Accident, the Other *Cock* had a Good Riddance of his Rival; took Possession of the Province they Contended for, and had All his Mistresses to Himself again.

The Moral.

A Wise, and a Generous Enemy will make a Modest Use of a Victory; for Fortune is Variable.

THE·FIGHTING·COCKS AND THE·EAGLE.

Fable LIX.

The Stag and the Fawn.

A *Fawn* was Reasoning the Matter with a *Stag*, why he should run away from the *Dogs* still; for, says he, you are Bigger and Stronger than They. If you have a Mind to stand, y'are better Arm'd; And then y'are Fleeter if you'll Run for't. I can't Imagine what should make you so Fearful of a Company of Pityful Curs. Nay, says the *Stag*, 'tis All True that you say, and 'tis no more than I say to my self Many *Times*, and yet whatever the Matter is, let me take up what Resolutions I please, when I hear the *Hounds* once, I cannot but betake my self to my Heels.

The Moral.

'Tis One thing to Know what we ought to do, and Another thing to Execute it; and to bring up our Practice to our Philosophy: He that is naturally a Coward is not to be made Valiant by Councel.

THE·STAG AND THE·FAWN.

Fable LX.

The Wasps and the Honey-Pot.

THere was a Whole Swarm of *Wasps* discovered an Overturned *Honey-Pot*, and there they Cloy'd and Clamm'd themselves, till there was no getting Away again; which brought them to Understand in the Conclusion, that they had pay'd too Dear for their Sweet-Meats.

The MORAL.

Loose Pleasures become Necessary to Us by the Frequent Use of them, and when they come once to be Habitual, there's no getting Clear again.

THE·WASPS AND THE·HONEY·POT·

Fable LXI.

The Fox and the Grapes.

THere was a Time, when a *Fox* would have Ventur'd as far for a Bunch of *Grapes*, as for a Shoulder of *Mutton*, and it was a *Fox* of Those days, and That Palate, that stood Gaping under a Vine, and licking his Lips at a most Delicious Cluster of Grapes that he had Spy'd out there; He fetch'd a Hundred and a Hundred Leaps at it, till at last, when he was as Weary as a Dog, and found that there was No Good to be done; *Hang 'em* (says He) *they are as Sour as Crabs;* and so away he went, turning off the Disappointment with a Jest.

The Moral.

'Tis Matter of Skill and Address, when a man cannot Honestly Compass what he would be at, to Appear Easy and Indifferent upon All Repulses and Disappointments.

THE·FOX AND THE·GRAPES.

FABLE LXII.

The Hare and the Tortoise.

WHat a Dull Heavy Creature (says a *Hare*) is This same *Tortoise* ! And yet (says the *Tortoise*) I'll run with you for a Wager. 'Twas *Done and Done*, and the *Fox*, by Consent, was to be the Judg. They started together, and the *Tortoise* kept Jogging on still, 'till he came to the End of the Course. The *Hare* lay'd himself down about Mid-way, and took a Nap; for, says he, I can fetch up the *Tortoise* when I please : But he Over-slept himself it seems, for when he came to wake, though he scudded away as fast as 'twas possible, the *Tortoise* got to the Post before him, and Won the Wager.

The MORAL.

Up and be Doing, *is an Edifying Text; for Action is the Bus'ness of Life, and there's no Thought of ever coming to the End of our Journey in time, if we Sleep by the Way.*

THE·HARE AND THE·TORTOISE·

Fable LXIII.

The Dog and the Cock upon a Journey.

A *Dog* and a *Cock* took a Journey together. The *Dog* Kennell'd in the Body of a Hollow Tree, and the *Cock* Roosted at night upon the Boughs. The *Cock* crow'd about Midnight; (at his Usual Hour) which brought a *Fox* that was abroad upon the Hunt, immediately to the Tree; and there he stood Licking of his Lips, at the *Cock*, and Wheedling him to get him Down. He Protested he never heard so Angelical a Voice since he was Born, and what would not He do now, to Hug the Creature that had given him so Admirable a Serenade! Pray, says the *Cock*, speak to the Porter below to open the Door, and I'll come Down to ye: The *Fox* did as he was Directed, and the *Dog* presently seiz'd and Worry'd him.

The Moral.

The Main Bus'ness of the World is Nothing but Sharping, and putting Tricks upon One Another by Turns.

THE·DOG·AND·THE·COCK
UPON·A·JOURNEY.

FABLE LXIV.

𝕿𝖍𝖊 𝖁𝖎𝖓𝖊 𝖆𝖓𝖉 𝖙𝖍𝖊 𝕲𝖔𝖆𝖙.

A *Goat* that was hard Press'd by the Huntsmen, took Sanctuary in a *Vineyard*, and there he lay Close, under the Covert of a *Vine*. So soon as he thought the Danger was Over, he fell presently to Browsing upon the Leaves; and whether it was the Rustling, or the Motion of the Boughs, that gave the Huntsmen an Occasion for a Stricter Search, is Uncertain: but a Search there was, and in the End he was Discover'd, and shot. He dy'd in fine, with this Conviction upon him, that his Punishment was Just, for offering Violence to his Protector.

The MORAL.

Ingratitude Perverts all the Measures of Religion and Society, by making it Dangerous to be Charitable and Good Natur'd.

THE·VINE AND THE·GOAT.

I

Fable LXV.
The Ass, the Lion, and the Cock.

AS a *Cock* and an *Ass* were Feeding together, up comes a *Lion* Open-Mouth toward the *Ass :* The *Cock* presently cries out ; Away Scoures the *Lion*, and the *Ass* after him : Now 'twas the Crowing of the *Cock* that Frighted the *Lion*, not the Braying of the *Ass*, as That Stupid Animal Vainly Fanci'd to Himself, for so soon as ever they were gotten out of the Hearing of the *Cock*, the *Lion* turn'd short upon him, and tore him to pieces, with These Words in his Mouth : Let never any Creature hereafter that has not the Courage of a Hare, Provoke a *Lion*.

The Moral.

The Force of Unaccountable Aversions, is Insuparable. The Fool that is Wise and Brave Only in his Own Conceit, runs on without Fear or Wit, but Noise does no Bus'ness.

THE·ASS·THE·LION AND·THE COCK·

Fable LXVI.

The Snake and the Crab.

THere was a Familiarity Contracted betwixt a *Snake* and a *Crab*. The *Crab* was a Plain Dealing Creature, that Advis'd his Companion to give over Shuffling and Doubling, and to Practice Good Faith. The *Snake* went on in his Old Way: So that the *Crab* finding that he would not Mend his Manners, set upon him in his Sleep, and Strangled him; and then looking upon him as he lay Dead at his Length: This had never befall'n ye, says he, if You had but Liv'd as Straight as You Dy'd.

The Moral.

There's Nothing more Agreeable in Conversation, then a Franke Open way of Dealing, and a Simplicity of Manners.

THE·SNAKE AND THE·CRAB.

Fable LXVII.

The Raven and the Swan.

A Raven had a Great Mind to be as *White* as a *Swan*, and fancy'd to Himself that the *Swan's* Beauty proceeded in a High Degree, from his often *Washing* and *Dyet*. The *Raven* upon this Quitted his Former Course of Life and Food, and betook himself to the *Lakes* and *Rivers :* But as the Water did him no Good at all for his Complexion, so the Experiment Cost him his Life too for want of Sustenance.

The Moral.

Natural Inclinations may be Moulded and Wrought upon by Good Councell and Discipline ; but there are Certain specifick Properties and Impressions, that are never to be Alter'd or Defac'd.

THE·RAVEN AND THE·SWAN.

Fable LXVIII.

The Ape and the Dolphin.

PEople were us'd in the Days of Old, to carry Gamesome _Puppies_ and _Apes_ with 'em to Sea, to pass away the Time withal. Now there was One of these _Apes_, it seems, aboard a Vessel that was cast away in a very great Storm. As the Men were Paddling for their Lives, and the _Ape_ for Company, a Certain _Dolphin_ that took him for a Man, got him upon his Back, and was making towards Land with him. He had him into a Safe Road call'd the _Pyræus_, and took occasion to Ask the _Ape_, whether he was an _Athenian_ or not? He told him Yes, and of a very Ancient Family there. Why then (says the _Dolphin_) You know _Pyræus_ : Oh! exceedingly well, says T'other (taking it for the Name of a Man). Why _Pyræus_ is my very Particular Good Frind. The _Dolphin_, upon This, had such an Indignation for the Impudence of the _Buffoon-Ape_, that he gave him the Slip from between his Legs, and there was an End of my very Good Friend, the _Athenian_.

The Moral.

Bragging, Lying, and Pretending, has Cost many a Man his Life and Estate.

THE·APE AND THE·DOLPHIN.

Fable LXIX.

The Fox and the Crab.

A *Fox* that was Sharp-set, Surpriz'd a *Crab*, as he lay out of the Sea upon the Sands, and Carry'd him away. The *Crab*, when he found that he was to be Eaten, Well (says he) This comes of Meddling where we have Nothing to do; for My Bus'ness lay at Sea, not upon the Land.

The Moral.

No Body Pities a Man for any Misfortune that Befalls him, in Matters out of his Way, Bus'ness, or Calling.

THE·FOX AND THE·CRAB.

Fable LXX.

The Shepherd and his Sheep.

IN Old time when *Sheep* fed like *Hogs* upon Acorns, a Shepherd drove his Flock into a Little Oak-Wood, spread his Coat under a Tree, and up he went to shake 'em down some Mast. The Sheep were so Keen upon the Acorns, that they Gobbled up now and then a Piece of the Coat along with 'em. When the Shepherd took Notice of it : What a Company of Ungrateful Wretches are you, says he, that Cloath all Other People that have No Relation to you, and yet Strip Your Master, that gives ye both Food and Protection !

The Moral.

The Belly has no Ears ; *and a Ravenous Appetite Guttles up wha.- ever is Before it, without any regard either to Things or Persons.*

THE SHEPHERD AND HIS SHEEP.

Fable LXXI.
The Peacock and the Magpie.

IN the Days of Old, the Birds liv'd at Random in a Lawless State of *Anarchy;* but in time they began to be Weary on't, and Mov'd for the Setting up of a King. The *Peacock* Valu'd himself upon his Gay Feathers, and put in for the Office: The Pretenders were heard, the Question Debated; and the Choice fell upon the Poll to King *Peacock:* The Vote was no sooner pass'd, but up stands a *Magpie* with a Speech in his Mouth to This Effect: *May it please your Majesty*, says he, *We should be glad to Know, in Case the* Eagle *should fall upon us in your Reign, as she has formerly done, how will you be able to Defend us?*

The Moral.

In the Bus'ness of either Erecting, or Changing a Government, it ought to be very well Consider'd before hand, what may be the Consequences, in case of such a Form, or such a Person.

THE·PEACOCK AND THE·MAGPIE.

Fable LXXII.

The Lion, the Ass, and the Fox.

THere was a Hunting-Match agreed upon betwixt a *Lion*, an *Ass*, and a *Fox*, and they were to go Equal Shares in the Booty. They ran down a Brave Stag, and the *Ass* was to Divide the Prey; which he did very Honestly and Innocently into Three Equal Parts, and left the *Lion* to take his Choice: Who never Minded the *Dividend*; but in a Rage Worry'd the *Ass*, and then bad the *Fox* Divide; who had the Wit to make Only One Share of the Whole, saving a Miserable Pittance that he Reserv'd for Himself. The *Lion* highly approv'd of his Way of Distribution; but Prethee *Reynard*, says he, who taught thee to Carve? Why truly says the *Fox*, I had an *Ass* to my Master; and it was His Folly made me Wise.

The MORAL.

There must be no Shares in Sovereignty. Court-Conscience is Policy. The Folly of One Man makes Another Man Wise; as one Man Grows Rich upon the Ruines of Another.

THE·LION·THE·ASS AND THE·FOX·
GOING·OUT·HUNTING·

Fable LXXIII.

The Kid and the Wolf.

AS a *Wolf* was passing by a Poor Country Cottage, a *Kid* spy'd him from the Roof; and sent a Hundred Curses along with him. Sirrah (says the *Wolf*) if I had ye out of your Castle, I'd make ye give Better Language.

The Moral.

A Coward in his Castle, makes a Great Deal more Bluster then a Man of Honour.

THE·KID AND THE·WOLF.

Fable LXXIV.
The Geese and the Cranes.

SOme Sports-men that were abroad upon Game, spy'd a Company of *Geese* and *Cranes* a Feeding together, and so made in upon 'em as fast as their Horses could carry them. The *Cranes* that were Light, took Wing immediately, and sav'd themselves, but the *Geese* were Taken; for they were Fat, and Heavy, and could not Shift so well as the Other.

The MORAL.

Light of Body and Light of Purse, comes much to a Case in Trouble-some Times; Only the One saves himself by his Activity, and the Other scapes because he is not worth the Taking.

THE · GEESE AND THE · CRANES.

Fable LXXV.

The Angler and the Little Fish.

AS an *Angler* was at his Sport, he had the Hap to Draw up *a very Little Fish* from among the Fry. The Poor Wretch begg'd heartily to be thrown in again; for, says he, I'm not come to my Growth yet, and if you'l let me alone till I am Bigger, Your Purchase will turn to a Better Account. Well! says the Man, but I'd rather have a Little Fish in Possession, then a Great One in Reversion.

The MORAL.

'Tis Wisdom to take what we May, while 'tis to be Had, even if it were but for Mortality sake.

THE·ANGLER AND THE·LITTLE·FISH.

Fable LXXVI.
𝕿𝖍𝖊 𝕭𝖚𝖑𝖑 𝖆𝖓𝖉 𝖙𝖍𝖊 𝕲𝖔𝖆𝖙.

A *Bull* that was Hard Press'd by a *Lion*, ran directly toward a Goat-Stall, to Save Himself. The *Goat* made Good the Door, and Head to Head Disputed the Passage with him. Well! says the *Bull*, with Indignation, If I had not a more Dangerous Enemy at my Heels, then I have Before me, I should soon Teach you the Difference betwixt the Force of a *Bull*, and of a *Goat*.

The Moral.

'*Tis no Time to Stand Quarrelling with Every Little Fellow, when Men of Power are Pursuing us upon the Heel to the very Death.*

THE BULL AND THE GOAT.

Fable LXXVII.

The Nurse and the Wolf.

AS a *Wolf* was Hunting up and down for his Supper, he pass'd by a Door where a Little Child was Bawling, and an Old Woman Chiding it. *Leave your Vixen-Tricks*, says the *Woman, or I'll throw ye to the Wolf.* The *Wolf* Over-heard her, and Waited a pretty While, in hope the *Woman* would be as good as her Word; but No Child coming, away goes the *Wolf* for That Bout. He took his Walk the Same Way again toward the Evening, and the Nurse he found had Chang'd her Note; for she was Then Muzzling, and Cokesing of it. *That's a Good Dear*, says she, *If the Wolf comes for My Child, We'll e'en Beat his Brains out.* The *Wolf* went Muttering away upon't. There's No Meddling with People, says he, that say One Thing and Mean Another.

The MORAL.

'Tis Fear more then Love that makes Good Men, as well as Good Children, and when Fair Words, and Good Councel will not Prevail upon us, we must be Frighted into our Duty.

THE·NURSE AND THE·WOLF.

FABLE LXXVIII.
The Tortoise and the Eagle.

A *Tortoise* was thinking with himself, how Irksome a sort of Life it was, to spend All his Days in a Hole, with a House upon his Head, when so many Other Creatures had the Liberty to Divert Themselves in the Free, Fresh Air, and to Ramble about at Pleasure. So that the Humor took him One Day, and he must needs get an *Eagle* to teach him to Fly. The *Eagle* would fain have put him off, and told him, 'twas a Thing against Nature, and Common Sense; but (according to the Freak of the Wilful Part of the World) the More the One was Against it, the More the Other was For it: And when the *Eagle* saw that the *Tortoise* would not be said *Nay*, she took him up a matter of *Steeple-high* into the Air, and there turn'd him Loose to shift for Himself. That is to say; she dropt him down, *Squab* upon a Rock, that Dash'd him to Pieces.

The MORAL.
Nothing can be either Safe, or Easy that's Unnatural.

THE · TORTOISE AND THE · EAGLE.

Fable LXXIX.
The Fox and the Frog.

A *Frog* came forth out of a Pond, and made Proclamation of his Skill in *Physick*. Pray, says the *Fox*, Begin with your Own Infirmities before you Meddle with other Peoples.

The Moral.
Physician Cure thy Self.

THE·FOX AND THE·FROG.

Fable LXXX.
The Mischievous Dog.

THere was a very Good *House-Dog*, but so Dangerous a Cur to Strangers, that his Master put a *Log of Wood* about his Neck, to Prevent him Running at and Biting People. The Dog took this *Log of Wood* for a Particular Mark of his Master's *Favour*, till One of his Companions shew'd him his Mistake. You are Mightily Out (says he) to take this for an Ornament, or a Token of Esteem, which is in truth, no Other then a Note of Infamy set upon you for your Ill Manners.

The Moral.

This may serve for an Admonition to Those that make a Glory of the Marks of their Shame, and Value themselves upon the Reputation of an Ill Character.

THE·MISCHIEVOUS·DOG.

Fable LXXXI.
The Peacock and the Crane.

AS a *Peacock* and a *Crane* were in Company together, the *Peacock* spreads his Tail, and Challenges the Other, to shew him such a Fan of Feathers. The *Crane*, upon This, Springs up into the Air, and calls to the *Peacock* to Follow him if he could. You brag of your Plumes, says he, that are fair indeed to the Eye, but no way Useful or Fit for any manner of Service.

The Moral.

Heaven has provided not only for our Necessities, but for our Delights and Pleasures too; but still the Blessings that are most Useful to us, must be preferr'd before the Ornaments of Beauty.

THE·PEACOCK AND THE·CRANE.

Fable LXXXII.

The Fox and the Tiger.

AS a Huntsman was upon the Chace, and the Beasts flying before him; Let Me alone, says a *Tiger*, and I'll put an end to This War my self: At which Word, he Advanced towards the Enemy in his Single Person. The Resolution was no sooner Taken, but he found himself Struck through the Body with an Arrow. He fasten'd upon it presently with his Teeth, and while he was Trying to Draw it out, a *Fox* Ask'd him, from what Bold Hand it was that he Receiv'd This Wound. I know Nothing of That, says the *Tiger*, but by the Circumstances, it should be a Man.

The Moral.

There's No Opposing Brutal Force to the Stratagems of Humane Reason.

THE·FOX AND THE·TIGER.

Fable LXXXIII.

The Lion and the Four Bulls.

THere was a Party of Four *Bulls* that Struck up a League to Keep and Feed together, and to be *One and All* in case of a Common Enemy. If the *Lion* could have Met with any of them Single, he would have done His Work, but so long as they Stuck to This Confederacy, there was No Dealing with them. They fell to Variance at last among Themselves: The *Lion* made his Advantage of it, and then with Great Ease he Gain'd his End.

The Moral.

This is to tell us the Advantage, the Necessity, and the Force of Union; And that Division brings Ruine.

THE·LION AND THE·FOUR·BULLS.

FABLE LXXXIV.
The Crow and the Pitcher.

A *Crow* that was Extream Thirsty, found a *Pitcher* with a Little Water in't, but it lay so Low he could not come at it. He try'd first to Break the Pot, and then to Overturn it, but it was both too Strong, and too Heavy for him. He Bethought Himself However of a Device at last that did his Bus'ness; which was, by Dropping a great many Little Pebbles into the Water, and Raising it That Way, till he had it within Reach.

The MORAL.

There is a Natural *Logick* in *Animals,* over and above the *Instinct* of their *Kinds.*

THE·CROW AND THE·PITCHER.

FABLE LXXXV.
The Man and his Goose.

A Certain Good Man had a Goose, that Laid him Golden Eggs, which could not be, he thought, without a Mine in the Belly of her. Upon This Presumption he Cut her up to Search for Hidden Treasure: But upon the Dissection found her just like *Other Geese*, and that the Hope of Getting more had betray'd him to the Loss of what he had in Possession.

The MORAL.

This is the Fate, Folly and Mischief of Vain Desires, and of an Immoderate Love of Riches. Content wants Nothing, and Covetousness brings Beggery.

THE⚜MAN AND HIS GOOSE⚜ ✿

Fable LXXXVI.

The Wanton Calf.

A Wanton *Calf* that had little else to do than to Frisk up and down in a Meadow, at Ease and Pleasure, came up to a Working *Ox* with a Thousand Reproaches in her Mouth; Bless me, says the *Calf*, what a Difference there is betwixt your Coat and Condition, and Mine! Why, What a Gall'd Nasty Neck have we here! Look ye, Mine's as Clean as a Penny, and as smooth as Silk I warrant ye. 'Tis a Slavish Life to be Yoak'd thus, and in Perpetual Labour. What would you give to be as Free and as Easy now as I am? The Ox kept These Things in his Thought, without One Word in Answer at present; but seeing the *Calf* taken up a While after for a *Sacrifice:* Well Sister, says he, and have not you Frisk'd fair now, when the Ease and Liberty you Valu'd your self upon, has brought you to This End?

The Moral.

'Tis No New Thing for Men of Liberty and Pleasure, to make Sport with the Plain, Honest Servants of their Prince and Country: But Mark the End on't, and while the One Labours in his Duty with a Good Conscience, the Other, like a Beast, is but Fatting up for the Shambles.

THE·WANTON·CALF.

FABLE LXXXVII.

The Leopard and the Fox.

AS a *Leopard* was Valuing himself upon the Lustre of his Party-colour'd-Skin, a Fox gave him a Jog, and Whisper'd him, that the Beauty of the Mind was an Excellence, Infinitely to be Preferr'd above That of a Painted Out-side.

The MORAL.

A Good Understanding is a Blessing Infinitely beyond All External Beauties.

THE·LEOPARD AND THE·FOX.

Fable LXXXVIII.

The Hawk and the Farmer.

A *Farmer* had the Fortune to take a *Hawk* in the Hot Pursuit of a *Pigeon*. The Hawk Pleaded for her self, that she never did the *Farmer* any Harm, and therefore I hope, says she, that You'l do Me None. Well! says the *Farmer*, and pray what Wrong did the *Pigeon* ever do you? Now by the Reason of your own Argument, you must e'en Expect to be Treated Your self, as You your self would have Treated This *Pigeon*.

The Moral.

'Tis good to Think before we Speak, for fear of Condemning our selves out of our Own Mouths.

THE·HAWK AND THE·FARMER.

M

Fable LXXXIX.
𝕿𝖍𝖊 𝕭𝖊𝖆𝖗 𝖆𝖓𝖉 𝖙𝖍𝖊 𝕭𝖊𝖊-𝕳𝖎𝖛𝖊𝖘.

A *Bear* was so Enrag'd once at the Stinging of a *Bee*, that he ran like Mad into the *Bee-Garden*, and Over-turn'd All the *Hives*, in Revenge. This Outrage brought them Out in Whole Troops upon him; and he came afterwards to Bethink himself, how much more Advisable it had been to Pass over One Injury, then by an Unprofitable Passion to Provoke a Thousand.

The Moral.

Better pass over an Affront from One Scoundrel, then draw the Whole Herd of the Mobile about a Man's Ears.

THE ✿ BEAR AND THE ✿ BEE-HIVES.

FABLE XC.
The Fatal Marriage.

A *Lion* that found himself Hamper'd in a Net, call'd to a *Mouse* that was passing by, to help him out of the Snare, and he'd never forget the Kindness, he said. The *Mouse* Gnaw'd the Threads to pieces, and when he had set the *Lion* at Liberty, desir'd him in Requital to give him his Daughter. The *Lion* was too Generous to Deny him Any thing, but most Unluckily, as the New Bride was just about to Step into the Marriage Bed, she happen'd to set her Foot upon her Husband at Unawares, and Crush'd him to Death.

The MORAL.

The Folly of an Inconsiderate Love. The Force of Gratitude, and Good Nature, and the Misery that Accompanies Unequal Matches.

THE·FATAL·MARRIAGE.

Fable XCI.

The Cat and the Mice.

AS a Company of *Mice* were Peeping out of their Holes for Discovery, they spy'd a *Cat* upon a Shelf; that lay and look'd so Demurely, as if there had been neither Life nor Soul in her. Well (says one of the *Mice*) That's a Good Natur'd Creature, I'll Warrant her; One may read it in her very Looks; and truly I have the Greatest Mind in the World to make an Acquaintance with her. So said, and so done; but so soon as ever *Puss* had her within Reach, she gave her to Understand, that the Face is not always the *Index* of the Mind.

The Moral.

'Tis a Hard Matter for a Man to be Honest and Safe ; for his very Charity and Good Nature Exposes, if it does not Betray him.

THE·CAT AND THE·MICE·

Fable XCII.

The Wild Boar and the Fox.

AS a *Boar* was Whetting his Teeth against a Tree, up comes a *Fox* to him. Pray what do you mean by That? (says he) for I see no Occasion for't. Well, says the *Boar*, but I do; for when I come once to be Set upon, 'twill be too Late for me to be Whetting, when I should be Fighting.

The Moral.

No Man, or State can be Safe in Peace, that is not always in readiness to Encounter an Enemy in Case of a War.

THE·WILD·BOAR AND THE·FOX.

FABLE XCIII.

The Porcupine and the Snakes.

SOme *Snakes* were prevail'd upon in a Cold Winter, to take a *Porcupine* into their Cell; but when he was Once in, the Place was so Narrow, that the Prickles of the *Porcupine* were very Troublesome to his Companions: so that the *Snakes* told him, he must needs Provide for Himself somewhere else, for the Hole was not Big enough to Hold them All. Why then, says the *Porcupine*, He that cannot *Stay* shall do Well to *Go:* But for my Own Part, I am e'en Content where I am, and if You be not so too, Y'are Free to Remove.

The MORAL.

Possession is Eleven Points of the Law.

THE·PORCUPINE AND THE·SNAKES

Fable XCIV.
The Hawk and the Nightingale.

AS a *Nightingale* was Singing in a Bush, down comes a Rascally Kite of a *Sparrow-Hawk*, and Whips her off the Bough: The Poor Wretch Pleaded for her self, that alas! her Little Carcass was not worth the While, and that there were Bigger Birds enough to be found. Well, says the *Hawk*, but am I so Mad d'ye think, as to Part with a Little Bird that I have, for a Great One that I have Not? Why then, says she, I'll give ye a Delicate Song for my Life: No, no, says the *Hawk*, I want for my Belly, not for my Ears.

The Moral.

A Bird in the Hand is Worth Two in the Bush.

THE·HAWK AND·THE NIGHTINGALE·

Fable XCV.
The Cat and the Fox.

THere was a Question started betwixt a *Fox* and a *Cat;* which of the Two could make the best Shift in the World, if they were put to a Pinch. For my own part, (says *Reynard,*) when the worst comes to the worst, I have a whole Budget of Tricks to come off with at last. At that very instant, up comes a Pack of Dogs full-Cry toward them. The *Cat* presently takes a Tree, and sees the Poor Fox torn to Pieces upon the very Spot. Well, (says *Puss* to her self,) One Sure Trick I find is better than a Hundred Slippery ones.

The MORAL.

Nature has provided better for us, than we could have done for our Selves.

THE·CAT AND THE·FOX.

Fable XCVI.

The Wolf, the Lamb, and the Goat.

A *Wolf* overheard a *Lamb* Bleating among the *Goats*. D'ye hear Little One, (says the *Wolf*,) if it be your Dam you want, she's yonder in the Field. Ay (says the Lamb,) but I am not looking for her that was my Mother for her *Own* sake, but for her that Nurses me up, and Suckles me out of *Pure Charity*, and *Good Nature*. Can any thing be Dearer to you, says the *Wolf*, than she that brought you forth? Very Right, says the Lamb; and without knowing or caring what she did: And pray, what did she bring me forth *for* too; but to Ease her self of a *Burden?* I am more Beholden to her that took Pity of me when I was in the World already, then to her that brought me into't, I know not how. 'Tis *Charity*, not *Nature*, or *Necessity* that does the Office of a *Tender Mother*.

The Moral.

There's a difference betwixt Reverence and Affection; the one goes to the Character, and the other to the Person, and so distinguishes Duty from Inclination. Our Mothers brought us into the World; a Stranger takes us up, and Preserves us in't. So that here's both a Friend and a Parent in the case, and the Obligation of the one, must not destroy the Respect I owe to the other; nor the Respect the Obligation: And none but an Enemy will advise us to quit either.

THE WOLF THE LAMB AND THE GOAT.

N

Fable XCVII.
The Cock and the Fox.

THere was a *Fox* set up near a *Hen-Roost*, to hold forth the Doctrin of Terror and Example. A *Cock* spy'd it, and scour'd away from't, as fast as his Legs and his Wings could carry him, and the Birds hooted at him for't. Hark ye my Masters, (says he,) there are *Live-Foxes* as well as *Dead* Ones, by the Token one of 'em had me by the Back but t'other day, and a Thousand Pound to a Nut-shell I had never got off again. And pray tell me now, if any of you had but been in my condition, whether the very Print of a *Foxes Foot* would not have started ye; and much more the Image of him in his *Skin*.

The MORAL.

The Burnt Child Dreads the Fire.

THE·COCK AND THE·FOX.

Fable XCVIII.

The Fox in the Well.

AN Unlucky *Fox* dropt into a Well, and cry'd out for Help: A *Wolf* overheard him, and looks down to see what the Matter was. Ah, (says *Reynard*,) Pray lend me your Hand Friend, or I'm lost else. *Poor Creature!* says the Wolf, *Why how comes this about? Prithee how long hast thou been here? Thou canst not but be mighty Cold sure.* Come, come, this is no Time for Fooling, says the *Fox;* set me upon *Terra Firma* first, and then I'll tell ye the History.

The MORAL.

When a Man is in Misery, there must be no Trifling in the Case. 'Tis a Barbarous Humour to stand Bantering out of Season. 'Tis no Time or Place for Raillery, when a Life's at Stake.

THE·FOX IN·THE WELL.

Fable XCIX.
The Ass Eating Thistles.

A Certain *Ass* (yet none so *Assish* as will presently appear) trudging laden with Cakes and Wine, Capons, and every jolly sort of Victual, for his Master and the Reapers to *Wag their Chops* upon, spy'd a Stout and Sturdy *Thistle*, and fell to with all the Stomach he was able.   Ha (says he) How many of those Lick-fingering Guzzling Trencher-scrapers, I warrant ye, would Skip and Fall a Merry-making at sight of the Curious Meats and Drinks that make up my Fardel!   Now this *Thistle*, which tickles my Leathery Palate so pleasantly, is to me worth a Score of those your Decked-out Dishes and insipid Comfitries!

The Moral.

What's Meat to one Man, is Nothing but a Tasteless Vanity to the Other. But He who knows what he likes, and takes no Shame in Owning it, even though an Ass's Skin Clothe him, has more Wit than many of his Neighbours.

THE·ASS·EATING·THISTLES.

Fable C.

The Wolf and the Lion.

THere was a *Wolf* had Seiz'd upon a *Sheep*, and Makes Off with it to his Den. On his way he had the Hap to meet with a *Lion*, come forth a-foraging, who without more Ado makes his Booty of the Carcass, and leaves the *Wolf* a-gaping. Why, how now (cries the *Wolf* in a rage) Ha' ye no Conscience, that ye rob Honest Folk on the King's Highway? The *Lion* he fell a-laughing, and Sirrah (says he) Would ye have me to believe, then, that your Proper Good Friend the *Shepherd* gave you the *Sheep?*

The MORAL.

A Rogue is Debarred from Appeal, when a Lustier Rogue than himself out-rogues him. To claim the Protection of Lawes Humane, we must first set ourselves to observe and maintain Them.

THE·WOLF AND THE·LION.